T0204918

School's in Session

By Elizabeth Dennis
Illustrations by Clarice Elliott

Ready-to-Read

SIMON SPOTLIGHT
An imprint of Simon & Schuster Children's Publishing Division
New York   London   Toronto   Sydney   New Delhi
1230 Avenue of the Americas, New York, New York 10020
This Simon Spotlight edition August 2024
Text copyright © 2024 by Simon & Schuster, LLC
Illustrations copyright © 2024 by Clarice Elliott
SIMON SPOTLIGHT, READY-TO-READ, and colophon are registered trademarks of Simon & Schuster, LLC.
Simon & Schuster: Celebrating 100 Years of Publishing in 2024
For information about special discounts for bulk purchases, please contact Simon & Schuster Special Sales at
1-866-506-1949 or business@simonandschuster.com.
Manufactured in the United States of America 0724 LAK
2 4 6 8 10 9 7 5 3 1
Library of Congress Cataloging-in-Publication Data
Names: Dennis, Elizabeth, author.
Title: School's in session! / By Elizabeth Dennis ; Illustrations by Clarice Elliott. Other titles: School is in session!
Description: New York City : Simon Spotlight, [2024] ∣ Series: Kids around the world ∣ Ready-to-read level 2 ∣
Summary: "Around the world, kids wake up and go to school every day, just like you! Some students go to
school by train, while others go by boat. There are schools in the middle of busy cities, and there are schools
that float on water. Learn all about what schools are like across the globe. Let's go to school!"— Provided by
publisher. Identifiers: LCCN 2023044176 (print) ∣ LCCN 2023044177 (ebook) ∣
ISBN 9781665957212 (hardcover) ∣ ISBN 9781665957205 (paperback) ∣ ISBN 9781665957229 (ebook)
Subjects: LCSH: Schools—Juvenile literature. ∣ School children—Transportation—Juvenile literature.
Classification: LCC LB1513.D46 2024 (print) ∣ LCC LB1513 (ebook) ∣ DDC 372.1042/1—dc23/eng/20231019 LC
record available at https://lccn.loc.gov/2023044176 LC ebook record available at https://lccn.loc.gov/2023044177

Glossary

Indigenous: relating to the earliest people known to live in a place

nomads: people who travel from place to place rather than living in one area

rickshaw: a small cart that is pulled by a person or powered by a motor

rural: relating to the countryside rather than the city

snowmobile: a motorized vehicle for one or two people that has steerable skis so it can travel on snow

zip line: a strong cable that is hung above a slope, to which a pulley and harness are attached for a rider

Note to readers: Some of these words may have more than one definition. The definitions above match how these words are used in this book.

Contents

Note to readers: Going to school is a unique experience for every student. Included in this book are just some examples of what school is like for kids around the world.

Chapter 1:
Let's Go to School!

Around the world, kids wake up and go to school, just like you. In many places kids ride on school buses or in cars, or they even walk to school. Some students take a train or a boat!

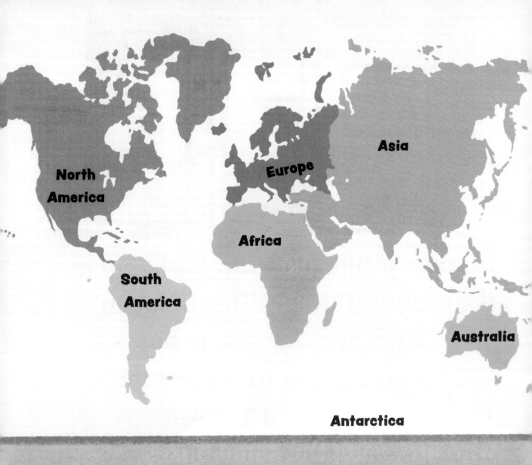

It's impossible to explore all the unique ways that kids go to school across the globe, but let's discover some of the amazing journeys kids take to go from where they live to where they learn.

In some places like New York City in the United States or Tokyo, Japan, some students take public buses and subway trains to get to school. They often sit next to grown-ups who are using the same buses and trains to get to work!

In Mackinac Island, Michigan,
it is so snowy in winter that
some students ride to school
on a **snowmobile**!
Brrr!

Some students ride in a
cable car to get to school
in Caracas, Venezuela!
Cable cars are useful in places
with narrow roads or many hills.

In a remote rainforest in Colombia, some students use a **zip line** to cross a huge canyon to get to school.

Many students around the world walk to school.

In Nigeria some students
walk three miles to get to school
in the morning, and then
three miles to get home at night.
That is six miles each day!

Six miles is greater than . . .

**the length of more than 80
football fields.**

In Thailand some students take
a motorized **rickshaw** to school.
These rickshaws are three-wheeled
vehicles that usually have open
sides. They are convenient
in places with a lot of traffic.

Students around the world have a lot in common: they chat with friends, study for tests, and listen to teachers. However they get to school, they are there to learn!

Chapter 2:
Class Is in Session

What do schools look like
around the world?
Some schools take place
in homes. Other schools are
in modern buildings.

In some places, schools are not
in buildings at all. . . .

In Bangladesh some schools
are on riverboats! This is because
there is a lot of flooding
in the area. There are also
floating libraries!

In India some schools travel to students who live outside of cities. Classes are held on train platforms or inside buses. Traveling schools bring kids together to learn!

In an area of Russia called
the republic of Sakha,
also called Yakutia,
there are schools for children
who are **nomads**.

These children are **Indigenous** (say: in-DIH-juh-nuss) people. They learn skills that are important to their culture, such as how to herd reindeer, make traditional crafts, and more!

In the Patagonia region of Argentina, some schools in **rural** areas have children of all ages in one classroom. The schools sometimes provide the only libraries for miles.

During the COVID-19 pandemic, many students had school at home. Some even went to forest schools, which meet outside and allow students to spend time in nature.

Can you imagine going to school in a forest, or on a bus, or on a boat that rocked during your math quiz?

Chapter 3:
Schoolwork and Play

Kids around the world spend
a lot of time learning in school . . .
but some students have
longer days than others.

Some high school students
in South Korea go to school
for over fourteen hours every day.
To catch up on sleep some students
in South Korea and Japan
might take naps during class.

Many elementary school students have seventy-five minutes of recess every day in Finland. After every hour or so, students get to take a fifteen-minute break to go outside.

They also have the shortest school day at just five hours long. Are you thinking of moving to Finland?

Ring! Ring!
That's the lunchtime bell! Many French students have two-hour lunch breaks, where they eat meals with meat, poultry, or fish, as well as a salad, cheese, dessert, and bread and butter on the side!

In Japan some students can harvest vegetables from school farms to be cooked in their school lunches.

Many kids around the world bring meals from home to school.

At the end of the day, most students have homework.

Countries with the least and most amounts of high school homework per week, on average:

Finland has the least amount of homework with 2.8 hours.

China has the most amount of homework with 13.8 hours.

How much homework do you have?

Whether by boat or by zip line,
kids around the world go to school
and learn and grow, just like you!

Every student's school experience is unique! What's your favorite thing about school?

Create Your Own School!

Take a piece of paper and draw your ideal imaginary school. Here are some questions to get you started:

If you could go to a school that wasn't in a building, what would it look like?

What kinds of unusual classes would you like to take there? What would the playground look like?

Would the cafeteria serve your favorite foods? Or would there be a farm where you grow your own vegetables?

Let's go to school!